W9-DHG-584

War Memorials

KOREAN WAR MEMORIAL

J.S. Burrows

ROURKE PUBLISHING

Vero Beach, Florida 32964

www.rourkepublishing.com

Photo credits: © US Department of Defense: Title Page, 5, 9, 14, 15, 19, 20, 21, 22, 24, 26, 27, 28; © US Navy: 6; © US Airforce: 7; © Wikipedia: 10; © NASA: 11; © Associated Press: 12, 13; © Ken Brown: 23; © David Kay: 25; © Emre Arican: border

Editor: Kelli Hicks

Cover and Interior design by Tara Raymo

Library of Congress Cataloging-in-Publication Data

Burrows, Jennifer.
  Korean War Memorial / Jennifer Burrows.
    p. cm. -- (War memorials)
  Includes index.
  ISBN 978-1-60694-426-4
  1. Korean War Veterans Memorial (Washington, D.C.)--Juvenile literature. 2.
Korean War, 1950-1953--Juvenile literature. 3. Washington (D.C.)--Buildings,
structures, etc.--Juvenile literature. I. Title.
  DS921.92.U6B87 2010
  951.904'26--dc22
                                    2009006014

Printed in the USA

CG/CG

www.rourkepublishing.com - rourke@rourkepublishing.com
Post Office Box 643328 Vero Beach, Florida 32964

TABLE OF CONTENTS

THE KOREAN WAR VETERANS MEMORIAL

After World War II, American soldiers were welcomed home with victory parades and celebrations. Eight years later, when the soldiers came home from the Korean War, hardly anyone noticed. They came home from the Forgotten War.

Over thirty years after the war, many people felt that the Korean War **veterans** deserved to be honored. The Korean War Veterans **Memorial** (KWVM) was built as a **tribute** to the American men and women who served in the Korean War.

The KWVM is located on the National Mall. The National Mall is two miles of land between the Lincoln Memorial and the Capitol in Washington, D.C.

OUR NATION HONORS
HER SONS AND DAUGHTERS
WHO ANSWERED THE CALL
TO DEFEND A COUNTRY
THEY NEVER KNEW
AND A PEOPLE
MET

One and a half million Americans served in the Korean War.

Following World War II, representatives from 50 countries met to form the United Nations. The group planned to work together to encourage peace in the world. The United States played an important role in forming that group.

On June 25, 1950, the Democratic Peoples Republic of Korea (North Korea) attacked the Republic of Korea (South Korea). The United States and other members of the United Nations decided to help South Korea.

For the United States, the Korean War was a fight against the spread of **Communism.** North Korea was a **Communist** country and South Korea was not.

Under the United Nations flag, Americans fought long and hard in Korea. After three years, one month, and two days, a **cease** fire ended the fighting, although neither side signed the agreement.

The United Nations successfully stopped the spread of Communism into South Korea. However, the relationship between North Korea and South Korea continues to be unstable and the two countries are openly hostile. The border between the two countries remains an unfriendly place.

The fighting during the Korean War was brutal from the day it started until the day it ended.

The veterans of the Vietnam War were honored with a memorial in 1982. This caused people to talk about building a memorial to honor the veterans of the Korean War as well.

In 1986, President Ronald Reagan signed a law that provided a spot for a memorial. He put together a team of 12 veterans to organize the project.

Lincoln Memorial

Korean War Veterans Memorial

The Korean War Veterans Memorial is in an area of the National

The team held a design contest and 500 artists entered. A group of **architects** from State College, Pennsylvania, won.

Some people liked the winning design, but others did not. This delayed construction of the memorial for a couple years. Changes to the design had to be made. Finally in 1993, construction began for the Korean War Veterans Memorial.

The Korean War Veterans Memorial cost 18 million dollars to build.
Most of the money came through private donations from Korean War
veterans. Two and one half million dollars came from South Korean
companies like Hyundai and Samsung.

13

In the middle of the memorial is a section called The Field of Service. It is 19 statues of American soldiers from the Korean War. They are made of gray, unpolished stainless steel and are over seven feet (two meters) tall.

The statues wear **ponchos** that appear to be whipping in a violent wind. In sunlight, the statues almost look alive. They look as if they are **cautiously** moving forward toward a flagpole.

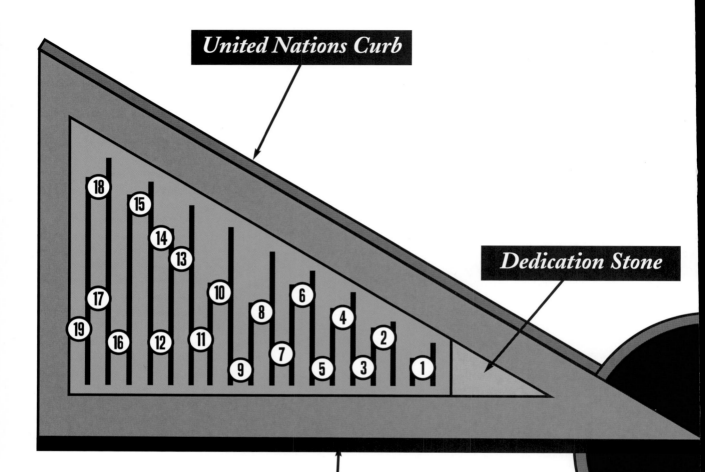

United Nations Curb

Dedication Stone

Mural Wall

Pool of Remembrance

The design of the memorial reflects the placement of soldiers and the importance of each individual job to the group as a whole unit.

POSITION	SERVICE	DUTY	RACE	WEAPON
1	Army	Lead Scout	Caucasian	M-1
2	Army	Scout	Caucasian	M-1
3	Army	Squad Leader	Caucasian	M-1
4	Army	BAR Gunner	African-American	BAR
5	Army	BAR Assistant Gunner	Caucasian	M-1/2 Carbine
6	Army	Rifleman	African-American	M-1 Garand Rifle
7	Army	Group Leader	Caucasian	M-1/2 Carbine
8	Army	Radio Operator	Caucasian	M-1/2 Carbine
9	Navy	Medical Corpsman	Hispanic	None
10	Army	Army Fwd Observer	Caucasian	M-1/2 Carbine
11	USAF	Air-Ground Controller	Caucasian	M-1/2 Carbine
12	USMC	Gunner	Caucasian	Machine Gun
13	USMC	Assistant Gunner	Caucasian	Tripod
14	USMC	Medical Corpsman	African-American	None
15	Army	Rifleman	Asian-American	M-1 Garand Rifle
16	Army	Rifleman	Caucasian	M-1 Garand Rifle
17	Army	Assistant Group Leader	Caucasian	M-1 Garand Rifle
18	Army	Rifleman	Hispanic	M-1 Garand Rifle
19	Army	Rifleman	American-Indian	M-1 Garand Rifle

The statues show soldiers representing the U.S. Army, Navy, Marine Corps, and Air Force working side by side to achieve success in battle.

On the ground around the statues there are strips of **granite** and Juniper bushes. The granite strips symbolize the difficult time the American soldiers had in Korea. The Juniper bushes are a symbol of the rough **landscape** in Korea.

A World War II veteran named Frank Gaylord sculpted the statues. Mr. Gaylord made the faces of the soldiers look worn out, but determined.

Ground troops did most of the fighting in the Korean War.

A shiny, black granite wall to the right of the statues is another part of the memorial. The wall is **etched** with over 2,400 smiling faces. The faces came from military photographs taken during the Korean War. From a distance, the outlines of the faces resemble the mountains of Korea. The wall has 41 sections and is 164 feet (50 meters) long.

A veteran named Louis Nelson designed the wall. He wanted to put pictures of our nation's soldiers on a **mantelpiece.** There are no names engraved on the wall. Friends and family often recognize the faces of their loved ones anyway.

FREEDOM IS NOT FREE

The Pool of Remembrance is a shallow body of water behind the flagpole. It is a quiet place for remembering the sacrifices of our American soldiers in Korea.

The pool is 30 feet (9 meters) across and the base is made of black granite. The surface of the water is as smooth as glass. A walkway, that represents Korea, sticks out into the middle of the pool.

A low granite **curb** to the left of the statues is also part of the memorial. The names of the 22 countries that helped South Korea are engraved on the curb. Seventeen nations provided troops and five provided medical support.

The Honor Roll lists the soldiers who died, were missing in action, or were captured as prisoners during the Korean War. The Honor Roll is on a computer data base at the memorial.

NO LONGER THE FORGOTTEN WAR

On a hot and muggy day in July, 1995, thousands of people gathered for the dedication of the Korean War Veterans Memorial. Many veterans present that day wore medals and symbols of their units in the military. Many old friends were reunited and remembered that afternoon.

It was a proud day for the veterans of the Korean War. Even extreme heat and a thunderstorm didn't dampen their spirits. Angus Deming, a Korean War veteran, called this day a long overdue celebration.

Each year thousands of people visit the Korean War Veterans Memorial. They come to honor our American heroes of the past, never to be forgotten again.

TIMELINE

1945 — The United Nations is formed.

1950 — North Korea attacks South Korea on June 25.

President Truman issues a public statement on June 27, and shorty after, the United States and the other countries in the United Nations enter the war.

1953 — A cease fire ends the fighting.

1982 — The Vietnam Veterans War Memorial is built.

1986 — President Ronald Reagan authorizes the KWVM.

1993 — Construction of the KWVM begins.

1995 — The KWVM is dedicated on July 27.

INTERESTING FACTS

The dedication of the KWVM was exactly 42 years after the fighting stopped in Korea.

Many states have memorials dedicated to their local Korean War veterans.

- ☆ On the State Capitol Grounds in Texas, there is a memorial made of granite with a bronze eagle on top.

- ☆ One memorial in New York, New York, has an outline of a soldier cut out of black granite.

- ☆ A memorial in Tallahassee, Florida, is a large, upright circle that is purposely broken at the top. The broken piece is stuck into the ground below.

- ☆ Springfield, Illinois, has a bronze bell mounted on a granite base as a memorial.

- ☆ In Santa Nella, California, there is a memorial inscribed with the names of the people from California who were lost in the Korean War.

GLOSSARY

architects (AR-ki-tekts): people who design buildings

cautiously (KAW-shuhss-lee): carefully

cease (seess): to stop

Communism (KOM-yuh-niz-uhm): a system of organizing a country so that the people share their resources under the government's control

Communist (KOM-yuh-nist): a person or group of people who follow Communism

curb (kurb): a raised border along the edge of a road

etched (echt): engraved

granite (GRAN-it): a type of rock

landscape (LAND-skape): a large area of land

mantelpiece (MAN-tuhl-peess): shelf above a fireplace

memorial (muh-MOR-ee-uhl): something built to help people remember a person or an event

peninsula (puh-NIN-suh-luh): land that is surrounded by water on three sides

ponchos (PON-chohs): a sleeveless raincoat with a hood

tribute (TRIB-yoot): something done to show respect

veterans (VET-ur-uhns): people who serve in the armed forces, especially during a war

INDEX

WEBSITES

www.koreanwar.org
www.nps.gov/kwvm/memorial/memorial.htm
www.abmc.gov/memorials/memorials/kr.php
tourofdc.org/monuments/KoreanWarMemorial
bensguide.gpo.gov/3-5/symbols/korea.html

ABOUT THE AUTHOR

J. S. Burrows is a former teacher who loves writing stories for children. She is deeply patriotic and thinks the men and women who serve in the military are heroes. When she's not writing, she enjoys cooking and playing Dance Dance Revolution with her three kids.